Horse Racing:

Gambling to Win

Bet & Win Like A Pro

By

Michael J. Haskett

A 'Special Report' in the continuing

"Make Money Enjoyably"™ series

© *2013 Durango Publishing Corp.*®

Published by: Durango Publishing Corp.®
Written by: Michael J. Haskett
www.DurangoPublishing.com
Email: books@DurangoPublishing.com

Other Titles By Durango Publishing

Mystery Series – Mike Shant
Policy Terminated
The Conversion
Lose Weight – While We Scam

Make Money Enjoyably Series
Vegas Pro's Best Racing Angles
Make to Make Big Money As An Information Publisher
How To Make Big Money Writing
Horse Racing: Gambling to Win

Fiction
The Day B.C. Quit Canada
The God Franchise

Special Reports
Horse Racing – 3 Year Olds
Writing – Daily Journal

Dedicated to all horseplayers everywhere, especially those who until now have had to ignore today's losses and look forward only to "tomorrow".
With this information "tomorrow" is here.

FREE BONUS –
SPECIAL REPORT: "3 year old racehorses are different—
And you should bet them differently."

Hello handicappers. If you would like to get my Special Report to increase your winning bets, you can get a FREE copy by clicking on the link below. But don´t delay, this FREE offer is only available for a limited time.

www.durangopublishing.com/racing-special-report-2/

Keep winning,
Michael J. Haskett

ABOUT THE AUTHOR

Michael J. Haskett started his career as a bush pilot flying in Canada´s Arctic. After a number of years flying commercially, he followed his entrepreneurial spirit and turned in his wings to become a full-time business owner. Over the past 3 decades he has established an extensive and varied sports and business background.

For many years he has also been a fan of horse racing, provided that a reasonable financial return can be earned in addition to the pleasure of seeing magnificent animals race. For almost as many years as a fan he has been able to keep his numbers in the black column. This current book details a complete mechanical system which can be easily put into practice by both neophytes and more experienced bettors. The author has personally bet at tracks in many countries, and now on the internet bets regularly at tracks in more than 18 countries. He is at work on a more specialized horseracing book for experienced bettors, under the working title "Vegas Pro Secrets". It should be ready for publication soon.

In addition to his duties/pleasures with the ponies, the author has developed, owned and operated a number of successful companies, was a business consultant for small to mid-size businesses, published information books and business documents ranging from web sites to extensive company operations manuals, and wrote (and marketed) a bestselling novel.

Readers interested in free updates for this book or the "Make Money Enjoyably" series can send their name and email address to books@DurangoPublishing.com. New titles will also be listed as published.

Table of Contents

Chapter 1

How to pick races to bet

The angles I'll show you here are the result of more than 45 years of experience and intensive research. Thousands of hours and thousands of dollars have been spent to locate, test, develop, and prove these angles. More than 24,000 races have been analyzed, one race at a time. The profitable angles identified in this Special Report represent **less than 2% of all the angles** checked and researched over those 45-plus years.

Without a spot angle system, and a

good wagering plan, **you might beat a race,**

but you can't beat the races.

More than half the battle in becoming

a winning horse race bettor is knowing

which races to bet, which to leave alone.

The rule is simple: Bet only those races in which the chances of winning, along with the close-to-race-time tote board odds, both combine to give you an edge.

For example: Say you figure the odds of your choice winning Race 5 are 1 in 4. Tote odds at 2 minutes to post are 5/2. Bet or not?

If you do bet races like that, you won't be in action long. The chances of losing (3 to 1) are reasonable, but combined with razor-thin odds (we never bet below 2/1, and that rarely; most of our bets will be at 4/1 or higher) this prescription probably

means red ink.

<u>So how do you determine which races</u>

<u>are worth betting?</u>

Step 1 is research. Keep records for a minimum of 3 to 4 weeks, or at least 30 races if you're not a regular at the track, OTB, or online. Make up a simple form, showing Type of Race (maiden, maiden claiming, claiming, allowance, handicap, stakes), and Results, based on standard $2 bet. If you bet more, as you'll have to in order to make any real money, just show your bet amount along with $2 ticket results. [Sample forms for this and other research needs are illustrated later in Chapter 7.]

Unsure exactly what the Race Type is? It will be identified for you on the racing form or program you use, right at the beginning of the Conditions which apply to that race: age, sex, number of races won this year, gross earnings last year, and similar conditions. These conditions are issued in the "Condition Book" issued by each track, usually once every two weeks.

Trainers and owners use these Condition Books to determine where best to enter their horses. Sometimes careful reading of the Conditions will let a bettor drastically eliminate several horses from a race; they may be considerably less skilled or even less ready than other entries. Yet many bettors never even consider the Conditions in their betting.

At the end of at least 30 races, separate the Results by Type of Race, and calculate your ROI for each Type of Race. ROI means Return on Investment. To calculate it, **divide $ won by $ bet**. If you won $200, and bet $160, your ROI = 1.25. If you won $120, but bet $150, your ROI = 0.8. Any figure below 1.0 is not good, and in this Special Report we'll strive for a minimum ROI of 1.2 or higher, which means if you bet enough you will profit handsomely. An instant and average 20% return on every $1 invested can <u>over time</u> make you financially independent.

If your ROI on a specific Type of Race <u>over time</u> is less than 1.1, throw out that Type.

Step 2 is continuing research.

Nothing anywhere, certainly in horse race betting, is carved in stone. Your initial research will show you which Race Types offer you the best rewards. For example, it's not unusual for some race players to do very well at one Race Type--say low priced claimers--but fail miserably at another Type, possible high class Allowance races.

The only way you will determine this information individually is by **your preliminary survey of your actual results**.

That information will let you get started on the right foot.

But don't expect those initial results to hold up forever. Almost everything at the track changes frequently, and what works for you today won't necessarily work tomorrow.

This simply means <u>you must continue to keep records</u>. Actually, for many race bettors, this aspect of their time at the track is quite pleasant. People who do well with horse betting often have temperaments and abilities that enjoy working with simple figures, especially when those figures can directly affect the money in their pockets.

But enjoy it or not, that material must be kept, preferably on a daily basis. It isn't complicated. **Use Form 1** (found in Chapter 7) or a similar form. After each race shows official results post your information; it won't take over a few minutes.

Step 3 is appraisal of your data.

Once each day, perhaps when you have time because you're not betting a race, go over your figures to determine which Type of Races you're doing well at, which are costing you money, and make changes in your future bets.

Keep these forms for each race meeting you follow at the track or an OTB location. If you bet at OTBs, where simulcasting now permits a bettor to choose from a dozen race tracks each day, keep a separate form for each track you follow. The results you get at Santa Anita won't likely match your results at Belmont or Turf Paradise.

Once the meet is over, all you need to do is transfer the summary information from your daily forms to a notebook. When the next meeting starts at your favorite track you'll already have some **valuable information to get you going**.

You'll want to keep up with new information, of course, and make modifications as needed. Remember, in horse race betting hard knowledge, unknown to the vast majority of part-time

bettors--and whose money you plan to take-

- is **pure gold.**

And always remember that for about

the last hundred years, at every track in the

US, Canada, England, France, Germany,

Japan, and other major thoroughbred racing

venues, **only about 4% of racehorse**

bettors have made consistent profits. Over

any reasonable period of time the other 96%

of bettors have lost. There is nothing more

ridiculous than the race track fan who

proudly proclaims "Today I won 5 out of 6

bets!" What he fails to add is that over the last 30, 50, 75, or even 500, race days, he has consistently lost money.

If you follow the simple selection and betting rules in this Special Report you will be able to join that elite 4% winners group. But to do that you'll have to keep sufficient records to show you **accurately and impartially** exactly what you're doing, how, and then with a modicum of investigative talent, why.

Always remember, too, that if these proven spot play angles don't turn up a good prospect in every race, or even very rarely on a day's program, there will be literally scores of races again tomorrow. Don't let panic force you into unprofitable bets.

Read on and join the winning group of horserace handicappers who really know what they're doing!

Chapter 2

A betting approach is only good if it will, over time, return to you more than you paid out.

Take this as gospel: <u>Never bet at odds under 2/1</u>. To do so regularly means that sooner or later you'll go bust. To make any money at under 2/1 odds ("chalk" odds to the knowledgeable), you have to win more than 40% of all races bet, and no one can do

that indefinitely.

You will **not bet under 3/1 odds** except when all factors are in your favor: type of race, some favorable change in addition to your normal System requirements (e.g.: a jock change from apprentice to one of the top 5 at the current meet), a major class change (dropping two levels on the claiming ladder), or some other significant factor which gives you an added edge.

(In all your betting, remember that you are **gambling against other bettors**, <u>not</u> the track or OTB. (The track or OTB takes a healthy cut of the overall betting pool before it is split among winners; they don't care who wins.) If you can find a piece of knowledge that most other bettors don't have, or understand why a certain change could mean an improved win chance, you will have an edge against your opponents. That is the very basis of this overall System: obtain knowledge which others don't have, and profit accordingly.)

Most of your bets under this System will be at a **minimum of 4/1**, sometimes much higher. Don't be afraid of high odds.

Sometimes they will be justified by the horse's real lack of winning chance. But frequently high odds will mean nothing more than:

(a) a local horse or jock favorite is running, and so much money is being dumped on him that the odds on other horses are higher than they should be; (b) you know something about the high-odds horse which most others don't.

Both of these situations can and not-too-infrequently will result in **whopping payoffs**. There's nothing quite like the thrill of seeing your 25/1-horse romp home as you calculated he would. It's a thrill that chalk players (those who bet favorites only) will never know.

Chapter 3

How to bet (win, place, or exotic)

Nowadays there are a wide variety of bets you can make on each single race. You can also make bets covering two races (Daily Double) or 5, 6, even 9 races, such as the Pick 6 or Pick 9, or whatever. These multiple-race bets are **exactly like buying a lottery ticket**. The odds against you winning are far higher, far more out of proportion, than are "normal" bets on one race.

If you want to "take a chance", by all means bet the Pick 6 or Pick 9. But don't expect this System--or any System, for that matter--to help you. There is absolutely no way a System can be used to pick the winners of 5 or more separate races. And that's why even track fans who have been betting for 20, 30, or more years, rarely if ever win such lottery tickets. There are just too many factors that work against you over a series of 5, let alone 9, races.

So our System will concentrate on

individual race bets, those that you can

reasonably expect to "beat" over time.

Most of our bets will be win bets.

There is usually simply too much of a

difference between win and place payoffs to

make the latter worthwhile. For example, a

$2 win bet on an 8/1 horse will pay about $18. Often, however, the place bet will return a disappointing $6 or even less, rather than the theoretically correct $9.

Occasionally we will bet to place when there is something doubtful about our pick's chances to get across the wire first. But the key word is <u>occasionally</u>.

Exotic bets? That means, in addition to the terrible-return multiple race bets described above, the quinellas and exactas now usually offered on each race.

Sometimes these can be a good deal. But again, so many inexperienced bettors now use these bets, without any real knowledge of what they're doing, that payoffs are usually below what they should be.

To determine if you should bet the quinella or the exacta, watch the tote board about two minutes to race time. For the same dollar amount bet, the exacta estimated payoff should be clearly a minimum of twice the estimated quinella payoff. If not, buy twice the number of tickets on the quinella. (An exacta ticket pays off only if you pick the first two horses across the line in the correct order. A quinella ("Q") pays if you pick the first two horses, regardless of order finish.)

The drawback today to exacta and quinella tickets it that too many bettors use them in an attempt to catch big payoffs from Longshots. They don't really know what they're doing, but they'll buy $2 exacta and/or quinella tickets on every longshot combination, in the hope that some will come in and pay off.

This means that often legitimate Qs or exactas you choose by our System will pay far less than they should, due to this unsophisticated random and quantity buying.

The only way to bet Qs and Exactas intelligently: pick your horse, using our System. Then use it to select a second choice. If the estimated payoffs on the tote screen appear to be sufficient, **then consider a small bet**. If the payoffs are below what you demand as return for the risk involved, use the money to bet on your System horse. To win, of course.

If you do want to back up your normal win bet with a place ticket as well, your best approach is to use a 3,1 formula: Bet $3 (or multiples, of course) on the nose for every $1 bet on the place position.

Show betting is for little old ladies of either sex. If you can't stand to bet to win, with an occasional place bet, you're better off giving up horse race betting completely. Try bingo, grandma.

Remember, too, that the tote board estimated payoffs on Qs and Exactas can and often are greatly affected by **big last minute bets** placed by knowledgeable bettors who wait until then so that the betting crowd won't see that they think they have a sure-fire winner or winners.

As with all bets, you are wise to <u>make your bets as close to race time as possible</u>. At many tracks this is a problem; understaffing means you have to get into line at least 5, maybe 10, minutes before post time. To a lesser degree the problem can exist at poorly managed OTBs.

At Las Vegas casinos, managed by intelligent people who realize the bettor is the customer, this is ordinarily not a problem at all, except possibly on Kentucky Derby or Breeder's Cup days, when everyone over the age of 15 becomes an instant racing fan for 1 or 2 days.

If you bet at home on your internet betting account, this last-minute betting is normally not a problem; you can normally get your bets in right up to the "Off" notice.

But as the internet has solved many former track and OTB minor problems, it has also made it even easier for big bettors to hold off until literally the last possible moment.

So that the horse you like and bet at 7/2 a few minutes before Post-time, may show up after the race is running, dropped down to 3/1, even 5/2 in extreme cases.

This condition will be more of a problem when you are betting tracks like Turf Paradise or many of the smaller Eastern tracks, where the betting pools are

usually much smaller than tracks like Santa
Anita or Belmont.

Chapter 4

How much to bet: Using the effective
Kelly Criterion formula

     Knowing how much to bet on each
race is a major key to making money over
time at the races. Fortunately for all of us a
man named Kelly solved this mathematical
problem some years ago, and nothing has
come along since which improves on his
original formula.

     The reasoning behind the formula is
fairly extensive. But you needn't worry

about the philosophy. Just learn the formula, and use it **with assurance that it does work.**

Every major winning horse race bettor uses the Kelly Criterion (KC) formula, or a variation very close to it.

<u>Here's the information you need to</u>

<u>put Kelly to work for you:</u>

Your winning % (what % of <u>all</u> <u>races</u> bet you win.) Using the information in this Special Report you can expect to average somewhere between 18 and 30%. (Each different Race Type will likely show a different Win % for you; check again Chapter 1.)

Your losing % (just subtract the above win % from 100%. If you win 26%, the figure here would be 100-26 = 74 %.)

Your average odds. Calculate this by this mini-formula:

Average odds = (Average $Won- Average $Bet) divided by Average $Bet.

If your records show that the average amount you won is $14--based as everything is in this Special Report on the standard $2 bet--and the average amount bet is $2, your average odds

$$= (14-2)/2 = 6 \text{ to } 1 \text{ odds.}$$

Now plug the figures into the Kelly formula, which is

Total winning % - (Total Losing % / average odds)

<u>Using the above example figs</u>:

26-(74 / 6) = 14%.

OK. What does that 14% figure mean?

Simply, your KC figure is about 14%, and **you should bet 14%** of your Total Bank next event. Remember that the KC should be applied to and used separately with each Race Type, so your KC can easily vary from as low as 4 or 6% on Race Types you don't do too well at, to perhaps 30 or even 35 or 40% on those Race Types you really cream. Follow the Kelly Criterion race betting approach and over time you will not go broke, according to Mr. Kelly's calculations, and you stand an excellent chance of substantially increasing your Total Bank amount.

Periodically, at least once a week, preferably after each day at the track, you should recalculate your Kelly figure. Do it separately for each Race Type you bet.

It usually won't move significantly, but it will move, and you want to be betting the correct formula figure. **Follow the KC formula and you won't go wrong**.

Chapter 5

The types of races (maiden, claimer, handicap, etc.)

Now we're getting to the good stuff.

Here we'll see which races should be bet.

The all-important rule is simple**: Bet only those races on which you can reasonably expect to score.**

Don't bet every race, or every type of race. If you do, you'll end up a loser.

MAIDEN CLAIMERS

These races are tough to beat because the horses by definition have never won an official race in their careers. And that means the Past Performance data won't be of great help. But here's an angle which has worked pretty well over the years:

• Bet only Maiden Claimers in which there are a **maximum of 3 first time starters** (no previous official races at all). If the race is open to both sexes, bet a male only. Your selection will have had a workout in the last 12 days, and at a distance within 1 furlong of today's race distance.

• If there is only one selection, bet him. If more than 1 choice, pass the race.

• Minimum odds should be 7/2.

This Race Type often has win payoffs in the clouds, because so many bettors haven't a clue as how to handicap horses who have run but a few if any races, and those without winning any. Or even worse, have never even raced before.

But if you follow the points above
you will over time benefit. Use the
minimum bet odds, but don't be afraid if
that number on your chosen horse gets well
into double digits.

MAIDEN

These horses are like Maiden Claimers; they have not won a single race, and in fact this may be their first official time on the race track. The horses are however not offered for sale (through the Claiming process, which is usually restricted to owners and trainers registered at that track).

While similar to Maiden Claiming races, the difference is that these horses are valued more highly by their owners and managers, although sometimes this is simply an opinion not grounded in any factual evidence.

Follow the same rules as for Maiden Claimers, as until the horse actually chalks up a win or at least gets into the money, the owner's/manager's opinions don't mean a great deal to intelligent bettors.

CLAIMING RACES

There is a good class drop angle here.

The rules are simple:

- Last race within 20 days, and horse beaten by a maximum of 10 lengths.
- Today's race distance must be within 1 furlong of last race, either longer or shorter.
- Today's purse value [not claiming price] must be down from last race.

- If 1 selection, bet it. If 2 or more choices, pass the race.

- Minimum odds should be 3/1 or higher.

ALLOWANCE RACES

This includes all types, from non-winners of 1 through non-winners of 4 races.

There must be a <u>minimum of 6 horses</u> in the race. If so, apply the following rules:

• From its last race add each horse's speed rating (+ variant if shown separately on the Past Performance figures you're using.) If one horse has a total figure 8 points higher than all other horses, that's your prime selection. **Minimum odds = 5/2**.

• If no horse has an 8-point advantage, look for one with a 5 point advantage. If so, that's a secondary selection. **Minimum odds = 7/2**.

• If no horse qualifies for prime or secondary selection, choose the horse with a 3-point advantage that was in the money (1st, 2nd, or 3rd) in his last race within 30 days. Minimum odds = **4/1.**

• If no horse qualifies at this point, pass the race.

STAKES & HANDICAP RACES

There are fewer of these than the above types but the payoffs can be very rewarding. Many bettors with little racing knowledge will pick a favorite horse in these big purse events, often choosing simply on the basis of liking a particular animal or a favored jockey who's riding it. If you choose intelligently you can expect to make good profits over time.

Here are some selection rules which can pay off big:

- In its last race the horse must have finished in the money.
- The last race must have been run within 45 days.
- If he won his last race, the horse must have won by 4 or more lengths.
- Minimum odds for a bet are 5/2. A prime bet requires at least 3/1.
- The horse must have had a workout within the previous 15 days. (Workout dates are

normally listed below the

horse's Past Performance data.)

Follow these simple selection and
betting rules and <u>over time</u> you will prosper,
realizing of course that on any one day, even
during any one race week, the races can go
against you. But persevere, and ***over time***
your ROI (Return on investment) should
exceed 1.2 (which simply—but very
profitably for you-- means $2.40 back for
every $2 you bet).

Chapter 6

Some bettors think that **jockeys** are a key factor in any race's decision. Undoubtedly a top earning jock <u>can</u> do a better riding job than an apprentice, but at any meet there will be several levels of jockeys, with the top 10 or so jocks probably winning about 50% or more of all races. When a jockey is hot, he can make a significant difference. The best way to handle jockeys is to keep records of them.

Use the form in Chapter 7. Keep it up to

date and you'll know far more than most

bettors at your track how important a

particular jock is to a specific kind of race.

Trainers are a very significant aspect

of horse race handicapping. They are the

final link between the horse and how it runs a specific race. Use the Trainer Records form in Chapter 7. <u>At least weekly update your records</u>. Within just a few weeks you'll see which trainer shows a healthy ROI on claiming races, which trainer loses badly in allowance races. Again, remember that you are wagering against **all other bettors** at your track, not the track or OTB. Keep and use your trainer forms and you'll have information few other handicappers will have.

Weight is highly overrated. Adding a few pounds to a horse weighing in at 800 or more pounds is like an average man carrying a half-pound package of cookies. It means perhaps less than a one-half percentage point of increased weight. That's significant? Sure, and the tooth fairy really exists.

Some trainers are overly concerned about weight (using an unskilled jock, for example, just to get a 5 lb. apprentice allowance) because they are lousy trainers to start with. Weight is something tangible they can understand, so they make a fuss about it. Better trainers realize that on a scale of 1-10 importance, 10 being tops, weight ranks right down there at about 1.

Equipment changes can be important, especially if used in conjunction with trainer records. For example, you may find that Trainer A doesn't do well with maiden claimers, except when he first puts blinkers on them. Then he racks up a 35% win rate. Similarly with adding special types of horseshoes or even bandages.

So when you keep your trainer

records it's a good idea to add a note when

he makes some equipment, bandage, or

legal drug change (adding Lasix, for

example) which gets good or bad results.

SUMMARY

You now have more information than the 95%+ of all horse race bettors who overtime end up in the red.

Keep your information records, and keep them up to date.

Use and apply the Kelly Criterion formula to calculate the amount to bet.

Use your information records to determine with what type of races you do best, and those with which you don't prosper.

Remember that that ROI of 1.2 is attainable, but not necessarily today. Maybe not even this week.

But follow these rules and you **will** join that exclusive group of horse race bettors who <u>overtime</u> show profits from your knowledge.

Watching well trained horseracing animals do what they do best is always pleasant.

Use this information to also make it profitable.

Chapter 7

Forms to use for your horse racing notes

[Simply add columns and lines as desired.]

[All based on the standard $2 bet]

Overall Track/OTB results for various

Race Types

Track
Date
Type of Race*
$ Bet
Result
$Won
Tot.$Bet
Tot.$ Won
Cumulative ROI
Type of Race = Maiden claiming, Maiden, Claiming, Allowance, Handicap, Stakes

TRAINER RECORDS

Trainer Name_____

Home Track_____

Across top:
$ Bet
$ Won
ROI
Changes*

Down left column:
Race Type
Maiden
Maiden Claiming
Claiming
Allowance
Handicap
Stakes

* Add details on equipment, drug, or bandage change information as relevant.

JOCKEY RECORDS

Jockey Name: _____

Home Track: _____

Race Type *:

$ Bet:

$ Won:

ROI:

Comments:

* Race Types

Maiden

Maiden claiming

Claiming

Allowance

Handicap

Stakes

The end of this book. Your start

as a winning horseplayer.

Dear Reader,

We are finding that on-line reviews are becoming an important part of our business. I wanted to ask if you could take a minute to write a review for us on Kindle (the link is below).

http://www.amazon.com/dp/B00CR2YQ0E

Thank you very much we really appreciate it...

Cheers,

Sam Martin, Promotion Manager

FREE BONUS –
SPECIAL REPORT: "3 year old racehorses are different— And you should bet them differently."

Hello handicappers. If you would like to get my Special Report to increase your winning bets, you can get a FREE copy by clicking on the link below. But don´t delay, this FREE offer is only available for a limited time.

www.durangopublishing.com/racing-special-report-2/

Keep winning,
Michael J. Haskett

Other Titles By Durango Publishing

www.ingramcontent.com/pod-product-compliance
Lightning Source LLC
Chambersburg PA
CBHW071422040426
42445CB00012BA/1264